SPOTTER'S GUIDE
DINOSAURS

David Norman
SCHOLASTIC INC.

New York   Toronto   London   Auckland   Sydney
Mexico City   New Delhi   Hong Kong   Buenos Aires

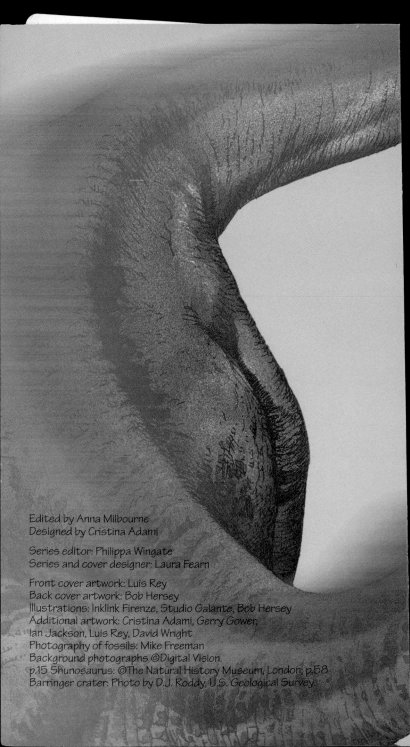

Edited by Anna Milbourne
Designed by Cristina Adami

Series editor: Philippa Wingate
Series and cover designer: Laura Fearn

Front cover artwork: Luis Rey
Back cover artwork: Bob Hersey
Illustrations: Inklink Firenze, Studio Galante, Bob Hersey
Additional artwork: Cristina Adami, Gerry Gower,
Ian Jackson, Luis Rey, David Wright
Photography of fossils: Mike Freeman
Background photographs ©Digital Vision.
p.15 Shunosaurus: ©The Natural History Museum, London; p.58
Barringer crater: Photo by D.J. Roddy, U.S. Geological Survey.

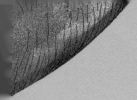

CONTENTS

HOW TO USE THIS BOOK

Dinosaurs are animals that are now extinct, which means they have all died out. This book is a guide to dinosaurs and other animals that lived millions of years ago. There are many museums you can visit to see dinosaur skeletons that scientists have found. Take this book with you if you go to a museum – it will help you imagine what these animals were like when they were alive.

PICTURES OF PREHISTORIC ANIMALS

The pictures in this book are based on the evidence scientists have found. They can learn a lot about a dinosaur by piecing together its remains to make a whole skeleton. They can work out its shape, how it moved and whether it walked on two legs or four. They can tell from its teeth whether it ate meat or plants. The only thing they cannot tell is the shade of a dinosaur's skin; so the skin shades in this book are imaginary.

An artist can build up a picture of a dinosaur using the shape of its skeleton.

PREHISTORIC ANIMAL NAMES

Many dinosaurs and other animals from this time have names ending in -*saurus*. This is a Greek word meaning *lizard*. It has been translated here as *reptile*, as this is closer to the truth. You can find out more about the group of animals to which dinosaurs and other prehistoric animals belong on page 8.

Dinosaurs have scientific names that describe them. For example, Velociraptor means *speedy reptile*. Under each scientific name, its meaning is shown in *italic* text.

There is a guide under each name to help you say it. For example, (<u>Tee</u>-lee-oh-<u>saw</u>-rus). Emphasize the parts that are underlined.

TIME SCALE

Each animal description shows a time scale like the one below. The shaded area shows when the animal lived. Scientists have divided time since Earth began into four eras. Each era is divided into periods. Dinosaurs lived between 225 and 65 million years ago in the Mesozoic era. This era is divided into three periods – Triassic, Jurassic and Cretaceous.

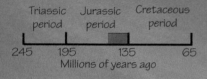

Triassic period — Jurassic period — Cretaceous period

245   195   135   65

Millions of years ago

PLACES

At the end of each animal description is the name of one or more countries or continents. This tells you where the remains of each animal have been found.

SIZE AND SHAPE

Each dinosaur or prehistoric animal in this book is measured from its head, down its backbone to the end of its tail. This measurement is known as the body length (BL).

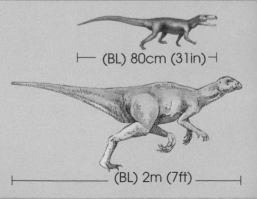

├── (BL) 80cm (31in) ──┤

├───── (BL) 2m (7ft) ─────┤

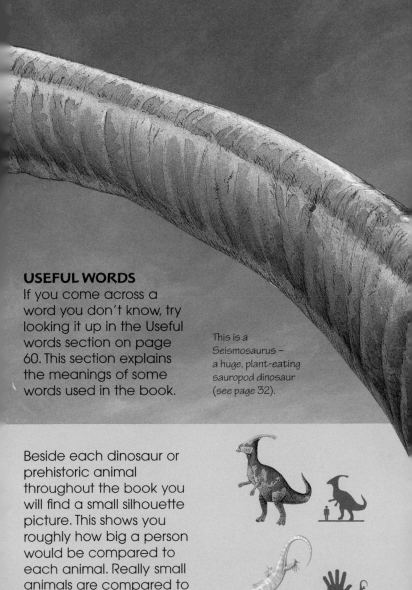

USEFUL WORDS

If you come across a word you don't know, try looking it up in the Useful words section on page 60. This section explains the meanings of some words used in the book.

This is a Seismosaurus – a huge, plant-eating sauropod dinosaur (see page 32).

Beside each dinosaur or prehistoric animal throughout the book you will find a small silhouette picture. This shows you roughly how big a person would be compared to each animal. Really small animals are compared to a person's hand.

WHAT ARE DINOSAURS?

A dinosaur is a type of reptile, although not the same as reptiles that are alive today. Dinosaurs belong to a group of animals called archosaurs. This group includes creatures that are well-known to us today, such as crocodiles and birds, as well as animals that are extinct, such as flying reptiles called pterosaurs. They all lay hard-shelled eggs and have scaly or feathered skin.

Archosaurs

All of these creatures are types of archosaurs.

Birds

Pterosaurs

Dinosaurs

Crocodiles

DINOSAUR LEGS

Dinosaurs differed from the rest of the archosaurs because of the way their legs were attached to their bodies. Animals like crocodiles have legs that are held out sideways from their bodies. Dinosaurs, on the other hand, had long, strong legs, which supported their bodies from underneath, like pillars. This meant that they could run faster, and also that they could grow to a bigger size, as legs arranged like this can hold more weight.

A dinosaur's legs support its body from beneath.

A crocodile's legs are held out to the sides.

9

TWO TYPES OF DINOSAURS

Dinosaurs are divided into two groups according to the shape of their hip bones. Dinosaurs are either "reptile-hipped" (called Saurischia), which means they had hips shaped like those of reptiles, or they are "bird-hipped" (called Ornithischia), which means they had hips shaped like those of birds. Strangely, birds today are related to reptile-hipped, not bird-hipped dinosaurs.

Apatosaurus –
a type of sauropod.

Plateosaurus –
a type of prosauropod.

Tarbosaurus –
a type of theropod.

Pentaceratops –
a type of ceratopian.

Scelidosaurus –
a type of ankylosaur.

Reptile-hipped dinosaurs

REPTILE-HIPPED

There were two main kinds of reptile-hipped dinosaurs – huge plant-eaters which walked on all fours (called **sauropods** and **prosauropods**) and meat-eaters which walked on two legs (called **theropods**).

BIRD-HIPPED

Bird-hipped dinosaurs were all plant-eaters. There were two-legged **ornithopods**, duck-billed dinosaurs (**hadrosaurs**), dome-headed dinosaurs (**pachycephalosaurs**), horned dinosaurs (**ceratopians**), plated dinosaurs (**stegosaurs**), and armoured dinosaurs (**ankylosaurs**).

Iguanodon – a type of ornithopod.

Parasaurolophus – a type of hadrosaur.

Stegosaurus – a type of stegosaur.

Stegoceras a type of pachycephalosaur.

Bird-hipped dinosaurs

TIME CHART

Era	Years ago	Period	Climate
Mesozoic	(million) 65	Cretaceous	Cool/variable
	135		Warm/dry
		Jurassic	Warm/dry
	195		
	245	Triassic	Hot/dry
Paleozoic	280	Permian	Warm/dry
			Cool
	345	Carboniferous	Glacial at South Pole
			Tropical
	395	Devonian	Warm/dry
	440	Silurian	Warm
	500	Ordovician	Cool/warm
	570	Cambrian	Cold

This chart shows how scientists have split time into eras and periods, and when some prehistoric animals lived.

Ornithomimus
Tyrannosaurus
Pinacosaurus
Triceratops
Corythosaurus
Pachycephalosaurus
Pteranodon
Deinonychus
Protoceratops
Iguanodon
Ceratosaurus
Brachiosaurus
Stegosaurus
Rhamphorhynchus
Archaeopteryx
Compsognathus
Megazostrodon
Lesothosaurus
Scelidosaurus
Plesiosaurus
Coelophysis
Plateosaurus
Euparkeria
Mixosaurus
Proterosuchus
Dicynodon
Diplocaulus
Seymouria
Dimetrodon
Hylonomus
Eusthenopteron
Ichthyostega
Dunkleosteus
Cladoselache
Sacabambaspis
Cup coral
Sea lily
Trilobite
Anomalocaris
Hallucigenia

13

WHAT ARE FOSSILS?

Fossils are the shapes or remains of animals and plants, preserved in rocks. Everything we know about dinosaurs is based on the study of their fossils.

HOW FOSSILS ARE FORMED

When animals die, their remains usually decay or are eaten. Fossils only form if the remains are quickly covered with sand or mud before this can happen. Over years, the mud or sand is compressed and turns into rock. The body of the animal decays, but the bones of the animal contain very tiny spaces, which gradually fill with minerals. This turns them (partly or wholly) into stone. Occasionally, the body of an animal or plant can be preserved without being turned into stone.

RARE REMAINS

Very rare other sorts of remains can be preserved. These might be teeth, eggs, footprint tracks, impressions of skin or even droppings.

1. Millions of years ago an animal died and fell into the sea.

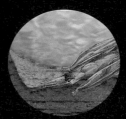

2. Its body sank to the sea bed, was covered in sand, and decayed.

3. Minerals filtered into the animal's bones and turned them into stone.

14

This is the fossil skeleton of a dinosaur called Shunosaurus. It was found in China.

FINDING FOSSILS

When the rock surface wears away, fossils can be uncovered. Fossilized bones can be dug out of the rock and pieced together to show what an animal looked like.

Remains of animals that have become extinct have also been found preserved in things other than rocks. In northern Siberia, mammoths have been found preserved in ice. The ice acted like a giant freezer.

15

CHANGING PLANET

The continents of the Earth may seem firm and solid but in fact they are moving very slowly all the time. This movement is called Continental Drift.

This shows the movement of the Earth's surface.

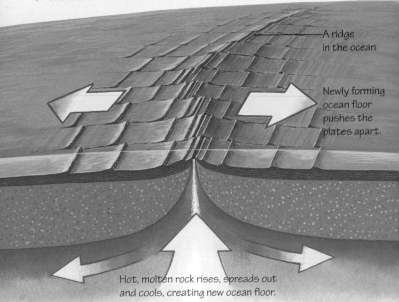

A ridge in the ocean

Newly forming ocean floor pushes the plates apart.

Hot, molten rock rises, spreads out and cools, creating new ocean floor.

The whole of the Earth's surface is divided up into giant sections, like a big jigsaw puzzle. These sections are called tectonic plates. Between the plates there are deep cracks (called trenches) and mountain ranges (called ridges).

At the ridges (either on the ocean floor or on land) molten rock rises from the core of the Earth. When it reaches the surface it cools and spreads out, forming new land or ocean floor. This pushes the plates outwards from the ridges.

This yellow line marks the position of a ridge in the ocean.

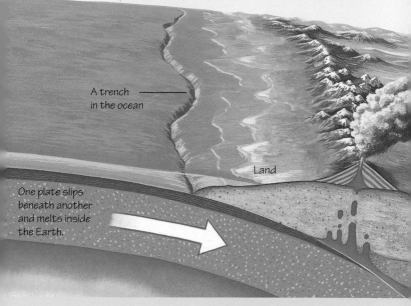

A trench in the ocean

Land

One plate slips beneath another and melts inside the Earth.

Since the Earth is not growing larger, there must also be areas where some of the ocean floor is disappearing. This happens at the trenches, where two tectonic plates are pushing against each other. One plate lifts and the other slips beneath it.

Over millions of years the continents have moved a long way. 200 million years ago, the coastlines of North and South America were joined to those of Africa and Europe. Since then, they have moved apart and are now separated by the Atlantic Ocean.

17

This shows how Earth has changed over millions of years. Dinosaur fossils can be found on land that has moved a long way since the dinosaurs were alive.

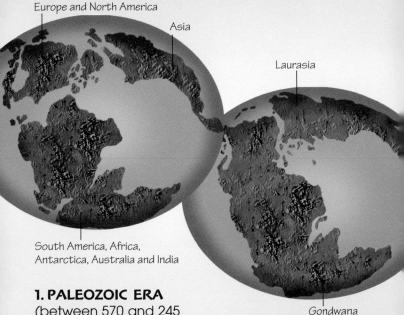

Europe and North America

Asia

Laurasia

South America, Africa, Antarctica, Australia and India

Gondwana

1. PALEOZOIC ERA
(between 570 and 245 million years ago)

The movements of the continents during this time are not well known. There seem to have been at least three big continental blocks – Europe and North America, Asia, and a third, made from all the other continents (South America, Africa, Antarctica, Australia and India).

2. MESOZOIC ERA – TRIASSIC PERIOD
(between 245 and 195 million years ago)

By this time, the three continental blocks had joined together to make one huge continent called Pangea. It had two major parts – Laurasia in the north and Gondwana in the south.

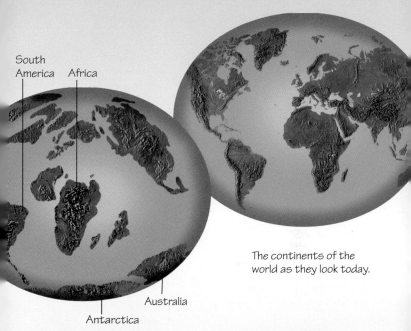

South America

Africa

Antarctica

Australia

The continents of the world as they look today.

3. MESOZOIC ERA – CRETACEOUS PERIOD
(between 135 and 65 million years ago)

In the Jurassic period, Pangea had started to split up. Gondwana had begun to separate from Laurasia. By early Cretaceous times they were separate. By the end of the Cretaceous period, Gondwana was breaking into today's continents – South America, Africa, India, Antarctica and Australia.

4. RECENT TIMES
(between 65 million years ago and the present day)

The continental blocks continued to divide and separate from one another. Eventually they arrived in the positions they are in today. One of the last separations that took place was that between North America and Europe.

EARLY FOSSILS

➡ CAMBRIAN SCENE

These are some of the earliest animals. Their fossils were found in rocks called the Burgess Shales in western Canada, and are about 530 million years old. Some animals look like ancient relatives of animals known today – such as a variety of worms; others are now extinct.

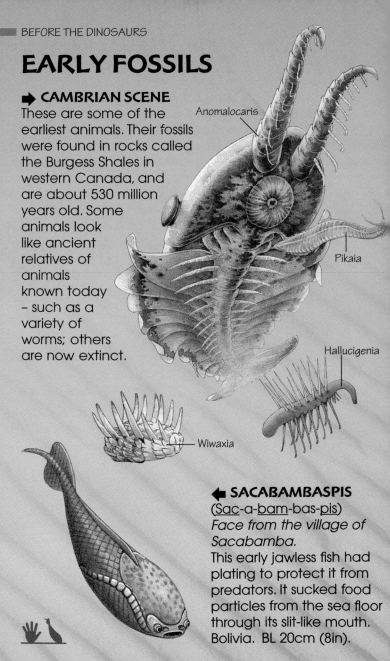

Anomalocaris

Pikaia

Hallucigenia

Wiwaxia

⬅ SACABAMBASPIS

(Sac-a-bam-bas-pis)
Face from the village of Sacabamba.
This early jawless fish had plating to protect it from predators. It sucked food particles from the sea floor through its slit-like mouth.
Bolivia. BL 20cm (8in).

JAWED FISH

◄ DUNKLEOSTEUS
(<u>Dun</u>-kel-<u>os</u>-tee-us)
Dunkle's bones
The largest early fish with
proper jaws. Its head alone
was 3m (10ft) long.
Having jaws meant
that it could open its
mouth wide. It ate
other fish. USA.
BL 10m (33ft).

➤ CLADOSELACHE
(<u>Cla</u>-doh-sell-<u>ah</u>-kee)
Ancestral shark
This early shark was similar
to today's sharks, except
for its large eyes and stiff
fins and tail. USA. BL 1m (3ft).

◄ EUSTHENOPTERON
(Yews-then-<u>op</u>-tur-on)
True narrow fin
This bony freshwater fish
had lungs as well as gills,
so it could gulp air from
the surface of shallow
water. It used its strong fins
to pull itself through
weed-choked swamps.
Greenland. BL 1m (3ft).

EARLY TETRAPODS

Any animal with four legs and a backbone is
called a tetrapod. Early tetrapods were like today's
amphibians – they could live on land and in water,
and most laid their eggs in the water.

◀ ICHTHYOSTEGA
(Ik-thee-oh-<u>stee</u>-ga)
Fish roof
One of the earliest animals
with legs and feet. It had a
scaled, fish-like body and
a tail fin. It used its front
legs to hold its head out
of the water to breathe.
It could walk on land but
spent most of its life in the
water. It ate fish.
Greenland. BL 1m (3ft).

➡ DIPLOCAULUS
(Dip-lo-<u>cawl</u>-us)
Double stalk
This animal had a
flattened body, small
legs and a long tail for
swimming. Its horns were
probably used as
stabilizers for swimming in
fast-flowing streams. USA.
BL 80cm (31in).

◀ SEYMOURIA
(See-<u>more</u>-ee-a)
From Seymour (Texas)
This animal's relatives laid
eggs in the water, which
hatched as tadpoles.
It lived mainly on land.
USA. BL 80cm (31in).

EARLY REPTILES

The early tetrapods developed into reptiles. They could now lay hard-shelled eggs, which did not dry out in the air. This meant that they could live permanently on land.

➡ HYLONOMUS
(<u>Hie</u>-lo-<u>noh</u>-mus) *In-tree mouse*
One of the first reptiles. Its body was lizard-like, with scaly skin. It ate insects. Canada. BL 10-20cm (4-8in).

⬅ DIMETRODON
(Die-<u>mee</u>-tro-don) *Two-sized tooth*
This was a flesh-eater with sharp teeth. The "sail" on its back helped to control its body temperature. USA. BL 3m (10ft).

➡ DICYNODON
(Die-<u>sine</u>-oh-don) *Two-dog tooth*
This pig-shaped animal was toothless, apart from two tusks in its top jaw. It ate plants. S. Africa. BL 1m (3ft).

⬅ LYCENOPS
(<u>Lie</u>-kay-nops) *Wolf-face*
This fierce flesh-eater had a slim, scaly body, long legs for chasing prey, and sharp teeth. S. Africa. BL1.5m (5ft).

23

EARLY ARCHOSAURS

The first archosaurs (see page 8) appeared in Permian times (about 260 million years ago). The first archosaurs were small, fast-moving animals with short backs, long necks and large heads with sharp, pointed teeth. Later, other archosaurs appeared, including animals like crocodiles, dinosaurs, pterosaurs and birds.

➡ PROTEROSUCHUS

(<u>Pro</u>-ter-oh-<u>soo</u>-kus)
Chasm reptile
A crocodile-like animal with a turned-down snout. It probably lived in water and ate fish. S. Africa. BL 2m (7ft).

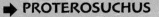

⬅ EUPARKERIA

(<u>You</u>-park-<u>eer</u>-ee-a)
Parker's true reptile
Crocodile-like, but it was purely a land animal. It caught smaller prey and ate dead animals it found. S. Africa. BL 80cm (31in).

➡ ORNITHOSUCHUS

(<u>Or</u>-nith-oh-<u>sook</u>-us)
Bird-like crocodile
This flesh-eater ran on its back legs, leaving its arms free to catch prey. It was similar to the first dinosaurs. Britain. BL 3m (10ft).

SMALL THEROPODS

Theropods were meat-eating dinosaurs with strong back legs and grasping hands for catching prey. The small theropods tended also to be very agile, fast-moving animals with small heads and long necks.

◀ EORAPTOR
(Your-<u>apt</u>-or)
Dawn predator
An early dinosaur. It had big eyes for finding its prey, and hooked claws for killing it. Argentina.
BL 2m (7ft).

➡ COMPSOGNATHUS
(Komp-sog-<u>nath</u>-us)
Pretty jaw
One of the smallest known dinosaurs. Fast-running meat-eaters such as this lived throughout the reign of the dinosaurs.
Germany. BL 60cm (2ff).

➡ COELOPHYSIS
(See-low-fi-sis)
Hollow face
It had a slender body with hollow bones, making it light and agile. It was ferocious and probably fed on small, plant-eating dinosaurs.
Mexico. BL 2m (7ft).

25

← COELURUS

(See-<u>lure</u>-us) *Hollow tail*
An agile meat-eater. It had
long arms with sharp claws
to catch prey. It may have
fed on Compsognathus
(page 25) and
Archaeopteryx (page 52).
Germany. BL 2m (7ft).

← VELOCIRAPTOR

(Vell-ossi-<u>rap</u>-tor)
Speedy predator
This animal ate reptiles and
mammals. An unusual fossil
was found of Velociraptor
fighting Protoceratops
(page 40) to the death.
Mongolia. BL 1.5m (5ft).

➡ DEINONYCHUS

(Die-<u>non</u>-ee-kus)
Terrible claw
The fiercest, fastest
flesh-eater. It leapt on prey,
taking it by surprise and
slashing with its large inner
claw. It may have hunted in
groups. USA. BL 2m (7ft).

LARGE THEROPODS

The largest theropods were a group called carnosaurs. Most carnosaurs had big heads, short necks and small arms. They killed their prey with their teeth or feet.

➡ DILOPHOSAURUS
(Die-<u>loaf</u>-oh-<u>saw</u>-rus)
Two-crested reptile.
This was one of the earliest carnosaurs. It had long, powerful legs and short arms. No one knows why it had the two crests on its head. USA. BL 6m (20ft).

⬅ ALLOSAURUS
(<u>Al</u>-oh-<u>saw</u>-rus)
Foreign reptile
This huge carnosaur hunted giant sauropods like Apatosaurus or Diplodocus (page 32). An Apatosaurus skeleton was found with Allosaurus toothmarks on it. N. America. BL 10m (33ft).

➡ SPINOSAURUS
(<u>Spine</u>-oh-<u>saw</u>-rus)
Spiny reptile
This unusual carnosaur had long spines (some up to 2m, or 7ft) forming a "sail" on its back. They helped to control its body temperature. Egypt. BL 8m (26ft).

◀ MEGALOSAURUS
(<u>Mega</u>-low-<u>saw</u>-rus)
Giant reptile
This was the first dinosaur ever to be named and decribed (1824). England. BL 6m (20ft).

◀ CERATOSAURUS
(Ser-<u>at</u>-oh-<u>saw</u>-rus)
Horned reptile
This carnosaur had a small horn on its head and bony ridges over its eyes. N. America. BL 6m (20ft).

➡ TYRANNOSAURUS
(Tie-<u>ran</u>-oh-<u>saw</u>-rus)
Tyrant reptile
One of the largest and last of the known theropods. It was taller than a giraffe, but was surprisingly light for its size. It tore its prey with its feet. Commonly known by its full name, Tyrannosaurus rex, this is the most famous meat-eater. USA. BL 15m (49ft).

Puny arms for its size

⬅ TARBOSAURUS
(<u>Tar</u>-bo-<u>saw</u>-rus)
Heroic reptile
This animal was similar to Tyrannosaurus. Many skeletons of this dinosaur have been found in recent years. Mongolia. BL 12m (39ft).

STRANGE THEROPODS

A variety of theropods with unexpected features have been discovered. Some of these dinosaurs show similarities to today's birds. This is no coincidence, as birds and theropods are close relatives.

➡ ORNITHOMIMUS
(Or-nith-oh-my-mus)
Bird imitator
It had a beak but no teeth (rare for a meat-eater). It ate insects, dinosaur eggs, fruit and mammals.
N.America, Asia.
BL 3-4m (10-13ft).

⬅ THERIZINOSAURUS
(Ther-iz-in-oh-saw-us)
Scythe reptile
A strange-looking animal with a hairy body. It had a small head and small teeth, but huge claws on its front legs and powerful back legs.
Mongolia. BL 6m (20ft).

➡ OVIRAPTOR
(Ov-ih-rap-tor) *Egg robber*
An odd animal, with a big crest above its nose and a strong, sharp beak.
Mongolia. BL 2m (7ft).

PROSAUROPODS

Prosauropods were medium to large plant-eating dinosaurs that lived in late Triassic times. They have the same ancestors as the huge plant-eating sauropods of the Jurassic period (page 32).

➡ RIOJASAURUS
(<u>Ree</u>-ok-a-<u>saw</u>-rus)
Reptile from Rioja, Argentina
A bulky, heavy plant-eater. It walked on all fours, supporting its great weight on massive, pillar-like legs and powerful feet.
Argentina. BL 7m (23ft).

⬅ PLATEOSAURUS
(Plat-ee-oh-<u>saw</u>-rus)
Flat reptile
This animal lived in herds. It walked on all fours, but could stand on its back legs to reach high leaves on trees. It had small, leaf-shaped teeth.
Germany. BL 6m (20ft).

31

SAUROPODS

Sauropods lived in Jurassic and Cretaceous times. They had huge bodies, long necks and even longer tails. They ate a wide range of plants, using their peg-like teeth to strip leaves off trees. They swallowed big stones to help crush up the food in their stomachs.

➡ DIPLODOCUS
(Dip-<u>lod</u>-oh-kus)
Double beam
This dinosaur was very long, with an extremely long tail, which it used like a whip to fend off enemies. It is not the longest known dinosaur, but one of the most complete skeletons yet found. N. America. BL 27m (89ft).

➡ APATOSAURUS
(A-<u>pat</u>-oh-<u>saw</u>-rus)
Headless reptile
Used to be known as Brontosaurus. Although shorter than Diplodocus, it was much heavier. N. America. BL 20m (66ft).

32

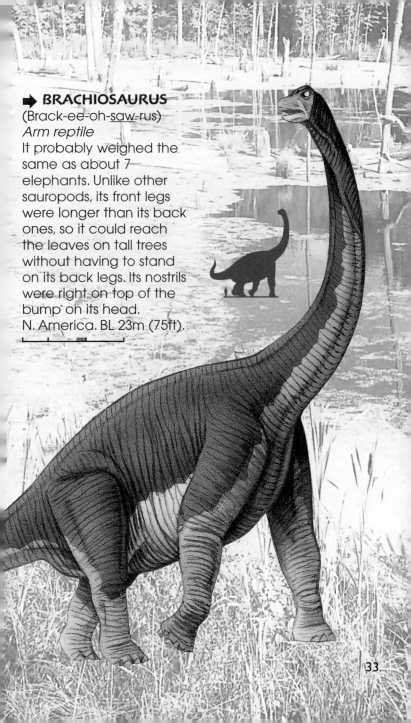

➡ BRACHIOSAURUS
(Brack-ee-oh-<u>saw</u>-rus)
Arm reptile
It probably weighed the same as about 7 elephants. Unlike other sauropods, its front legs were longer than its back ones, so it could reach the leaves on tall trees without having to stand on its back legs. Its nostrils were right on top of the bump on its head.
N. America. BL 23m (75ft).

ORNITHOPODS

Ornithopods walked mainly on their back legs. They had feet and hard beaks similar to those of birds. They were plant-eaters, and had cheeks to help contain their food when chewing.

← LESOTHOSAURUS

(Less-<u>oh</u>-toe-<u>saw</u>-rus)
Reptile from Lesotho
This was not a true ornithopod, as it had no cheeks, but it is closely related to all ornithopods. S.Africa. BL 90cm (35in).

← HETERODONTOSAURUS

(Het-er-oh-<u>don</u>-toe-<u>saw</u>-rus)
Mixed-tooth reptile
It was light and fast. It had tusks in its jaws to defend itself against enemies like Coelophysis (page 25). S. Africa. BL 90cm (35in).

➡ HYPSILOPHODON

(Hip-see-<u>loaf</u>-oh-<u>don</u>)
High-ridged tooth
One of the smallest, fastest dinosaurs. It used its stiff tail to balance when running. Britain, N. America. BL 2m (7ft).

34

◀ CAMPTOSAURUS
(Camp-toe-<u>saw</u>-rus)
Flexible reptile
This animal had claws on its hands and a pointed thumb spike. When chased, it ran on its back legs; when feeding on small shrubs, it moved on all fours. N. America, Britain. BL 5m (16ft).

➡ IGUANODON
(Ig-<u>wa</u>-no-<u>don</u>)
Iguana tooth
It had very powerful back legs. A sharp claw on each thumb was probably used as a weapon against enemies. The other fingers had hooves, so it could walk on all fours. Europe, N. America. BL 10m (33ft).

DUCK-BILLED DINOSAURS

Duck-billed dinosaurs (or hadrosaurs) descended from animals like Iguanodon (page 35). They lived in late Cretaceous times. Their top jaw was flat at the tip, a little like a duck's bill. They had small, closely packed teeth for grinding tough, woody plants. Most duck-billed dinosaurs had similar bodies, but their heads were very different shapes.

◀ OURANOSAURUS

(Oo-<u>ran</u>-oh-<u>saw</u>-rus)
Valiant reptile
This dinosaur was related to the duck-bills, as it had a beak. However, it wasn't a true duck-bill. It had thumb spikes like Iguanodon. The spines on its back may have been supported by a hump (like a camel's), which helped control body temperature. Niger. BL 6m (20ft).

➡ EDMONTOSAURUS

(Ed-<u>mon</u>-toe-<u>saw</u>-rus)
Reptile from Edmonton
This duck-bill had four fingers on its hands (no thumb spikes). It lived in large herds for protection and ate a variety of plants. A surprisingly fast runner on its strong back legs. Canada.
BL 10m (33ft).

← KRITOSAURUS
(Krit-oh-<u>saw</u>-rus)
Reptile from Kirtland
This duck-bill had a flat head with a hump on its nose. This may have been used for butting rivals during the mating season. USA. BL 10m (33ft).

➡ SAUROLOPHUS
(Saw-rol-<u>oh</u>-fus)
Ridged reptile
It had a prong on the back of its head. One suggestion is that this supported inflatable nose pouches so that the animal could bellow at rivals. N. America, Mongolia. BL10m (33ft).

← TSINTAOSAURUS
(<u>Sin</u>-ta-oh-<u>saw</u>-rus)
Reptile from Tsintao
Some scientists think it had a long spike on top of its head. This could have been used as a weapon, as well as to support its nose pouches. China. BL 10m (33ft).

← ANATOTITAN

(An-<u>a</u>-toe-<u>ti</u>-tan) *Big duck*
Thought to be one of the last
dinosaurs, this duck-bill had a
wide beak and probably
made honking noises.
N. America. BL13m (43ft).

← CORYTHOSAURUS

(Ko-<u>rith</u>-oh-<u>saw</u>-rus)
Helmeted reptile
Passages inside this
animal's crest may have
helped it to make honking
noises. Individuals of a herd
recognized each other by
their crest shapes.
N. America. BL 10m (33ft).

→ PARASAUROLOPHUS

(Para-<u>saw</u>-ro-<u>loh</u>-fus)
*Reptile with
parallel-sided crest*
Its crest was hollow with
air passages inside.
These probably helped
make its honking noises
louder. N. America.
BL 10m (33ft).

DOME-HEADED DINOSAURS

Dome-headed dinosaurs (or pachycephalosaurs) were closely related to ornithopods (page 34). They had similar bodies and were also bird-hipped plant-eaters. However, the dome of their skulls was extraordinarily thick. They lived in late Cretaceous times.

➡ STEGOCERAS
(Steg-<u>oss</u>-er-ass)
Horn roof
Remains are rare, as it probably lived in the uplands, where few fossils are ever preserved. It is quite possible that it lived as mountain sheep do today. N. America, BL 3m (10ft).

➡ PACHYCEPHALOSAURUS
(Pack-ee-<u>sef</u>-al-oh-<u>saw</u>-rus)
Thick-headed reptile
The dome on its head was very thick and surrounded by bumps and spikes. Some scientists think it had head-butting contests; others think they used their domes to recognize one another. Canada. BL 8m (26ft).

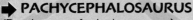

HORNED DINOSAURS

These horned dinosaurs with parrot-like beaks are called ceratopians. They lived in late Cretaceous times. Most of them can be recognized by the shape of their horns or neck frill.

➡ PSITTACOSAURUS
(<u>Sit</u>-ak-oh-<u>saw</u>-rus)
Parrot reptile
It had a hooked beak on its top jaw. It walked on its back legs, ate plants and probably used its clawed hands for digging. Mongolia. BL 2m.

⬅ PROTOCERATOPS
(<u>Pro</u>-toe-<u>ser</u>-a-tops)
First horned face
It had a big frill on the back of its head. It used its large, hooked beak for slicing leaves off tough plants. Mongolia. BL 2m.

Nests of Proceratops' eggs were found, with fossil fragments of baby dinosaurs that had died before hatching. The eggs were found arranged in a circle. Mongolia.

40

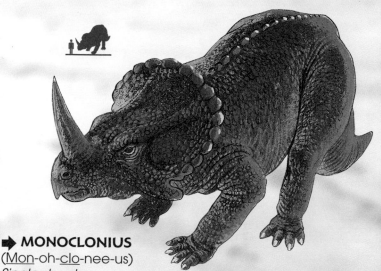

➡ MONOCLONIUS
(<u>Mon</u>-oh-<u>clo</u>-nee-us)
Single shoot
This animal looked similar to a rhinoceros of today. It had a single horn on its nose, and small eyebrow ridges. It lived in herds. N. America. BL 8m.

⬇ PENTACERATOPS
(<u>Pent</u>-ah-<u>ser</u>-a-tops)
Five-horned face
Its large frill extended half-way down its back. Apart from its nose and eyebrow horns, it also had two pointed cheekbones, like horns, beneath its eyes.
N. America. BL 7m.

41

➡ PACHYRHINOSAURUS
(Pack-ee-<u>rye</u>-no-<u>saw</u>-rus)
Thick-nosed reptile
A hornless ceratopian with a short frill. It had thick bone on top of its nose between its eyes. Canada. BL 4m (13ft).

⬅ LEPTOCERATOPS
(<u>Lep</u>-toe-<u>ser</u>-a-tops)
Slender-horned face
An unusual, small ceratopian that ran on its back legs. Its frill was small and it had no horns, as it could run away from predators, rather than trying to defend itself. N. America. BL 2m (7ft).

⬇ TRICERATOPS
(Try-<u>ser</u>-a-tops)
Three-horned face
The largest ceratopian and one of the last. It was about the same weight as 2 elephants. N. America. BL 11m (36ft).

PLATED DINOSAURS

Plated dinosaurs, or stegosaurs, were big plant-eaters whose remains have been found in rocks of Jurassic and early Cretaceous times as far apart as N. America, Europe, Africa and China. They can be easily recognized by the high, plate-like (or sometimes pointed) bones running in rows down their backs. Their tails ended in large, vicious-looking spines.

➡ KENTROSAURUS
(<u>Ken</u>-tro-<u>saw</u>-rus)
Prickly reptile
In danger, it would probably have turned its back on a predator. The spiky tail would have made attacking it difficult. Tanzania. BL 5m (16ft).

⬇ STEGOSAURUS
(<u>Steg</u>-oh-<u>saw</u>-rus)
Roofed reptile
The largest known stegosaur. It was thought that the plates on its back were for protection. Now experts believe that they were used for regulating body temperature. N. America. BL 8m (26ft).

ARMOURED DINOSAURS

These were medium to large, slow-moving plant-eaters. They are found through much of the dinosaur era – from the early Jurassic to the end of the Cretaceous period. They are called ankylosaurs (*fused reptiles*) because of their bony plating.

➡ SCELIDOSAURUS
(Skell-<u>id</u>-oh-<u>saw</u>-rus)
Limb reptile
One of the earliest armoured dinosaurs. It had a heavily plated back and head, and fed on plants.
England. BL 4m (13ft).

⬅ POLACANTHUS
(<u>Poll</u>-a-<u>can</u>-thus)
Many-spined
This dinosaur had shield-like plating over its hips and the top of its head. It also had many spines on its back. Isle of Wight. BL 4m (13ft).

➡ PINACOSAURUS
(Pee-<u>nah</u>-co-<u>saw</u>-rus)
Spiky reptile
Thick, flexible plates covered its head, neck, back and tail, protecting it against carnosaurs. Mongolia. BL 4.5m (15ft).

➡ EUOPLOCEPHALUS
(<u>Yew</u>-oh-plo-<u>sef</u>-al-us)
True-plated head
It had heavy, bony plating and lumps on its skin. Thick bone covered its head, like a helmet. Its belly was soft and unprotected. It probably used its tail like a club to defend itself.
N. America. BL 7m (23ft).

⬅ NODOSAURUS
(<u>Noh</u>-doh-<u>saw</u>-rus)
Lumpy reptile
It had bands of bony lumps across its back. These acted as protective plating. It does not seem to have had a tail club like other armoured dinosaurs.
N. America.   BL 6m (20ft).

➡ PANOPLOSAURUS
(<u>Pan</u>-oh-plo-<u>saw</u>-rus)
All-armoured reptile
It had simple leaf-shaped teeth and its jaw ended in a hard, toothless beak. It had spikes along its sides and across the back of its neck.
N. America. BL 7m (23ft).

FLYING REPTILES

Pterosaurs were light, fragile reptiles that flew. Their wings were leathery pieces of skin stretched along their long fourth finger. They seem to have evolved from early dinosaurs such as Eoraptor (see page 25).

➡ SHAROVIPTERYX
(Shah-roh-<u>vip</u>-tur-iks)
Sharov's wing
An early gliding reptile, similar to pterosaurs. It glided between branches using skin stretched between its tail and legs. Kazakhstan. BL 20cm (8in).

⬅ DIMORPHODON
(Die-<u>more</u>-foe-don)
Two types of tooth
One of the first pterosaurs. Its wing span was about 1m (3ft). Most of its wing was supported by its long end finger. England. BL 40cm (16in).

➡ RHAMPHORHYNCHUS
(<u>Ram</u>-foe-<u>rin</u>-kus)
Beak-nose
It swooped low over the sea, spearing fish with sharp, forward-pointing teeth. Its large eyes helped it to spot fish. Germany. BL 30cm (1ft).

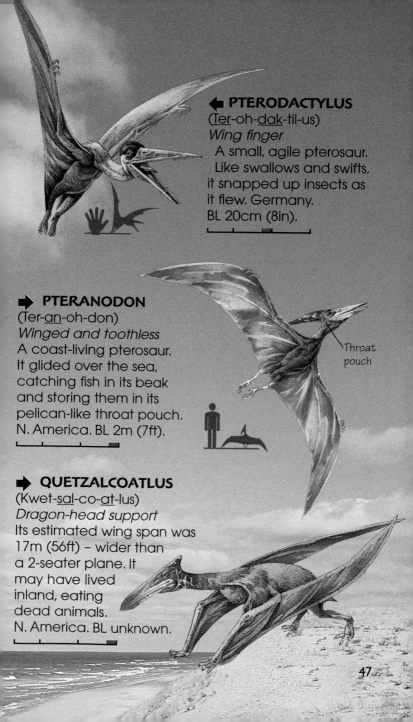

← PTERODACTYLUS
(<u>Ter</u>-oh-<u>dak</u>-til-us)
Wing finger
   A small, agile pterosaur.
Like swallows and swifts,
it snapped up insects as
it flew. Germany.
BL 20cm (8in).

➡ PTERANODON
(Ter-<u>an</u>-oh-don)
Winged and toothless
A coast-living pterosaur.
It glided over the sea,
catching fish in its beak
and storing them in its
pelican-like throat pouch.
N. America. BL 2m (7ft).

Throat
pouch

➡ QUETZALCOATLUS
(Kwet-<u>sal</u>-co-<u>at</u>-lus)
Dragon-head support
Its estimated wing span was
17m (56ft) – wider than
a 2-seater plane. It
may have lived
inland, eating
dead animals.
N. America. BL unknown.

47

PHYTOSAURS AND CROCODILES

Phytosaurs were early, crocodile-like archosaurs that lived at the end of the Triassic period. Today's crocodiles and alligators are related to animals that lived millions of years ago, such as Protosuchus, an early crocodile. Unlike today's crocodiles, these early crocodiles lived mainly on land.

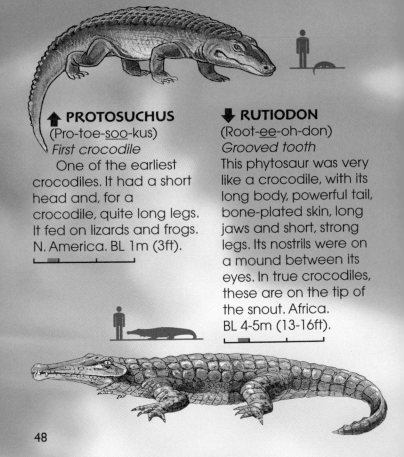

⬆ PROTOSUCHUS
(Pro-toe-<u>soo</u>-kus)
First crocodile
One of the earliest crocodiles. It had a short head and, for a crocodile, quite long legs. It fed on lizards and frogs. N. America. BL 1m (3ft).

⬇ RUTIODON
(Root-<u>ee</u>-oh-don)
Grooved tooth
This phytosaur was very like a crocodile, with its long body, powerful tail, bone-plated skin, long jaws and short, strong legs. Its nostrils were on a mound between its eyes. In true crocodiles, these are on the tip of the snout. Africa. BL 4-5m (13-16ft).

← METRIORHYNCHUS
(<u>Met</u>-ree-oh-<u>rin</u>-kus)
Long nose
It lived in the sea, unlike most crocodiles, which live in rivers. It had sharp teeth for catching fish, and swam using its tail and webbed feet. England. BL 4m (13ft).

← TELEOSAURUS
(<u>Tee</u>-lee-oh-<u>saw</u>-rus)
Tail reptile
This crocodile lived near estuaries and ate fish. It was not as good a swimmer as Metriorhynchus, as it had no tail flipper. Europe, Africa. BL 4m (13ft).

→ BERNISSARTIA
(<u>Bur</u>-nee-<u>sar</u>-tee-ah)
Crocodile from Bernissartia
This crocodile's blunt teeth show it may have fed on shellfish or dead animals. Belgium, England. BL 60cm (2ft).

← DEINOSUCHUS
(<u>Die</u>-no-<u>soo</u>-kus)
Terrible crocodile
This crocodile's head was over 2m (7ft) long. So far, only its skull has been found. N. America. BL unknown.

49

SWIMMING REPTILES

Several kinds of sea-dwelling animals lived in the Mesozoic era, at the same time as the dinosaurs. Ichthyosaurs looked similar to today's fish and dolphins. Plesiosaurs, pliosaurs and nothosaurs were less fish-like.

➡ MIXOSAURUS
(<u>Mix</u>-oh-<u>saw</u>-rus)
Mixed reptile
One of the first ichthyosaurs. Its tail had a fish-like fin and it used its legs as paddles. It had many sharp teeth for catching fish. Europe. BL 2-3m (7-10ft).

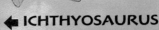

◀ ICHTHYOSAURUS
(Ik-thee-oh-<u>saw</u>-rus)
Fish reptile
This ichthyosaur's tail was like that of a fish. It swam by lashing its tail from side to side, and it balanced and steered with its flippers. Europe. BL 1-8m (3-26ft).

➡ OPHTHALMOSAURUS
(Off-<u>thal</u>-mow-<u>saw</u>-rus)
Eye reptile
An ichthyosaur with big eyes for seeing underwater. It ate squid-like animals whole, as it had no teeth. Europe. BL 4-5m (13-16ft).

➡ NOTHOSAURUS

(<u>No</u>-thow-<u>saw</u>-rus)
Southern reptile
This nothosaur lived in the sea, but came ashore to lay eggs. It caught fish with its sharp teeth. Europe, Asia, Africa. BL 3m (10ft).

➡ PLESIOSAURUS

(<u>Plees</u>-ee-oh-<u>saw</u>-rus)
Ribbon reptile
This plesiosaur swam slowly, flapping its flippers like a turtle. Fossilized stomach contents show that it ate squid-like creatures called belemnites as well as fish. Europe. BL 2-9m (7-30ft).

⬅ LIOPLEURODON

(<u>lie</u>-oh-<u>ploor</u>-oh-don)
Smooth-sided tooth
This was a ferocious pliosaur which ate large turtles, plesiosaurs and other sea reptiles. It swam by flapping its flippers. Australia. BL 13m (43ft).

THE EARLIEST BIRD

New discoveries in China prove that birds are the living descendants of theropod dinosaurs. Some theropods had fluff or feathers covering their bodies. The first true bird was Archaeopteryx.

➡ ARCHAEOPTERYX
(Are-kee-<u>op</u>-tur-iks)
Ancient wing
This early bird may have had to climb trees to launch itself into the air. Today's birds evolved from this one. Europe. BL 20cm (8in).

⬅ SINOSAUROPTERYX
(<u>Sine</u>-oh-saw-<u>op</u>-ter-iks)
Chinese reptile bird
This small dinosaur had fluff covering its body. It was similar to Compsognathus (page 25). China. BL 60cm (2ft).

⬅ CAUDIPTERYX
(<u>Cor</u>-dip-ter-<u>iks</u>) *Tail wing*
As well as having fluff on its body to keep it warm, this small dinosaur also had feathers on its tail and arms. It could not fly. China. BL 80cm (31in).

THE EARLIEST MAMMAL

Today's mammals are related to creatures like Dimetrodon (page 23) which lived before dinosaurs were alive. By the early Triassic period creatures that looked more mammal-like started to appear. They looked quite similar to dogs or rats.

← CYNOGNATHUS

(Sine-og-nath-us) *Dog jaw*
This wasn't a mammal, but looked like a dog. Like mammals, it had several different types of teeth (a reptile's teeth are usually all the same). Africa.
BL 2m (7ft).

→ THRINAXODON

(Thrin-axe-oh-don)
Trident tooth
This was not a mammal, but was even more mammal-like than Cynognathus. It had teeth of different kinds, whiskers on its nose, and was probably hairy like a mammal. S.Africa.
BL 40cm (16in).

← MEGAZOSTRODON

(Meg-ah-zost-ro-don)
Big girdle tooth
The earliest known mammal. It was hairy and gave birth to young. It was like a shrew and ate insects. S.Africa.
BL 6-8cm (2-3in).

FOSSILS

Fossils are hugely important in gathering information about prehistoric life. This section shows types of fossils that have been found.

➡ FOSSIL FERN
Fern fronds are often found in rocks from Carboniferous times. They are common plants of this period, often found alongside early tetrapods.

◀ CUP CORAL
These early corals lived in cup-shaped limestone on the sea floor. They were the oldest coral animals, living before and right through the age of dinosaurs. Now they are replaced by reef corals.

➡ BRACHIOPODS
(<u>Brack</u>-ee-oh-pods)
Lampshells
These are common fossils, found in rocks from early Cambrian to recent times. Attached by a stalk to the sea bed, the shell housed an animal which filtered food from the water.

➡ GASTROPODS

Gastropods are animals with simple shells, like snails. They have been common since Cambrian times. The shells in which they lived were various shapes – coiled, spiral-shaped, or cone-shaped.

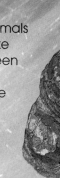

➡ BIVALVES

Bivalves have two shells hinged together, in which an animal lives (or lived). Cockles, mussels and razor shells are bivalves. Bivalves are very common fossils. In some cases, great lumps of rock are made entirely of broken bivalve shells.

⬅ AMMONITE

Ammonites were related to animals like snails and octopuses. Many ammonites lived in the sea until late Cretaceous times, then died out. The coiled shell contained chambers filled with air, which helped the animal to float.

➡ TRILOBITE
(<u>Try</u>-low-bite)
Three-lobed
Trilobites lived from
Cambrian to Triassic
times. They had hard
shells and many-
jointed legs. Most
trilobites found food
on the sea floor.

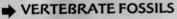

⬅ CRINOID
(<u>Crin</u>-oyd) *Sea lily*
Sea lilies are related
to sea urchins and
starfish. Attached to the
sea floor by a stalk, they
used their long tentacles
to catch tiny bits of food
(plankton) from the water.

➡ VERTEBRATE FOSSILS
Fossils of backboned
animals that lived
on land or in the
air are rarer than
those of sea
animals. Sometimes
a complete
skeleton is
discovered, but usually just
an odd tooth or bone is
found. These can be
difficult to identify.

This is a fossil
skeleton of
Seymouria
(page 22).

LIVING FOSSILS

Some modern-day animals look like living examples of prehistoric animals. Some have developed very little, and some have not changed since prehistoric times.

➡ TUATARA
This is a relative of lizard-like animals from Triassic times. It lives on islands near New Zealand. It looks nearly the same as its relatives did 200 million years ago.

⬅ PEARLY NAUTILUS
A rare, distant, living relative of squids, octopuses and extinct ammonites (page 55). It lives in a coiled shell which helps it to float in water. It lives in the Indian Ocean.

➡ COELACANTH
(see-la-canth)
Hollow spine
A big, predatory fish that lives in the Indian Ocean. It is closely related to Eusthenopteron (page 21).

➡ BRACHIOPODS
Brachiopods (also page 54) can be traced back to Cambrian times. An animal lives inside two hinged shells, which are attached to the sea floor by a stalk.

WHY DID THE DINOSAURS DIE OUT?

Fossil dinosaurs have been found in rocks from the Mesozoic era. But there are none in rocks that are newer than this. This shows that dinosaurs became extinct 65 million years ago, at the end of the Mesozoic era. Scientists think that dinosaurs died out because something violent suddenly changed the Earth's climate. Here are two explanations of what may have happened.

VOLCANIC THEORY

65 million years ago there were some huge volcanic eruptions in what is now India. Any animals close to the eruptions were killed immediately. Dust and gases from these volcanoes blocked out the sunlight and the world became cold and dark. Without sunlight all the plants died. The cold may have been enough to kill the dinosaurs, or they may have starved to death.

IMPACT THEORY

Many scientists think that a huge lump of rock from space, called an asteroid, hit the Earth. The asteroid was probably about 10km (6 miles) across. Yucatan in Mexico could be the place the asteroid hit, as a crater 200km (125 miles) wide has been found there. In the same way as described in the volcanic theory, vast clouds of dust and gas filled the air all around the world. Sunlight was blocked out so the Earth became cold, and plants then animals died.

This huge crater in Arizona was made by an asteroid hitting the Earth.

SURVIVORS

Many animals including birds, mammals, insects and sea creatures survived after the dinosaurs died out. Why some animals survived while others died is still a mystery.

USEFUL WORDS

This page explains some of the words used in the book. Words in *italic* text are explained separately.

amphibian – a backboned, usually four-legged animal that lays jelly-covered eggs in water. Examples include frogs and newts.

archosaur – a group of *reptiles* that includes crocodiles, birds, dinosaurs and pterosaurs.

descendant – an animal which is believed to have *evolved* from another animal.

evolution – the process by which many scientists believe types of plants and animals gradually, over millions of years, alter and become better suited to living in a particular environment.

extinct – died out. An animal is extinct if there are no animals of that type left alive.

fossil – the remains or impression of a dead plant or animal, preserved in rock.

mammal – a backboned, usually four-legged animal that gives birth to babies which are fed on their mother's milk. Examples include humans, mice, bats, horses and whales.

predator – an animal that kills and eats other animals.

prey – an animal that is hunted and killed by another animal.

prehistoric – before history started being written down by humans.

related – belongs to the same group of animals. For example, lions and tigers are related.

reptile – a backboned, usually four-legged animal which has a scaly skin and lays shelled eggs on land. Examples include lizards, snakes, tortoises, crocodiles, dinosaurs, pterosaurs.

tetrapod – any animal with four legs and a backbone.

WEß SITES TO VISIT

You can find lots of information about dinosaurs online. Here are some Web sites to visit:

DinoTreker – Contains great pictures and amazing models of dinosaurs.
http://www.dinotreker.com

Dino Don.Com – A site set up by a dinosaur expert named Don Lesser. It's full of great information and activities.
http://www.dinodon.com

Quia! Matching Game – A dinosaur game where you have to match the name of a dinosaur with its description.
http://www.quia.com

Natural History Museum, London – Dinosaur facts and figures.
http://www.nhm.ac.uk/ education/online/dinosaur _data_files.html

Children's Museum of Indianapolis – Information about different dinosaurs, with pictures you can print out.

http://www.childrens museum.org/kinetosaur/ sitemap.html

Walking with Dinosaurs (BBC Online) – Includes fantastic video clips, information and links to other dinosaur sites.
http://www.bbc.co.uk/ dinosaurs

University of Bristol Dinosaur Web Site – Dinosaur lists, references, research and pictures.
http://palaeo.gly.bris.ac.uk/ dinobase/dinomenu.html

American Museum of Natural History – Information for enthusiasts of all ages.
http://www.amnh.org/ exhibitions

National Geographic – Takes you on a dinosaur egg hunt.
http://www.national geographic.com/features/ 96/dinoeggs

MUSEUM GUIDE

Many museums around the world have exhibits of skeletons, models of dinosaurs, fossils and other prehistoric exhibits. Here are some examples:

UK
The Natural History Museum, London;
University Museum of Natural History, Oxford;
The Sedgwick Museum, University of Cambridge;
Ulster Museum, Belfast;
The Royal Museum of Scotland, Edinburgh;
Museum of Isle of Wight Geology, Isle of Wight.

USA
American Museum of Natural History, New York;
Carnegie Museum of Natural History, Pittsburgh, PA;
Dinosaur National Monument, Vernal, UT;
Field Museum of Natural History, Chicago, IL;
Museum of Paleontology, Berkeley, University of California, CA;
Museum of the Rockies, Bozeman, MT;
National Museum of Natural History, Smithsonian Institution, Washington D.C.;
Peabody Museum of National History, Yale University, New Haven, CT.

CANADA
Canadian National Museum of Natural Sciences, Ottawa;
Royal Ontario Museum, Toronto;
The Royal Tyrell Museum of Paleontology, Alberta.

AUSTRALIA
Museum Victoria, Melbourne;
Australian Museum, Sydney;
Queensland Museum, Brisbane.

CONTINENTAL EUROPE
Belgium: Institut royal des Sciences naturelles de Belgique, Brussels;
France: Muséum National d'Histoire Naturelle, Paris;
Germany: Museum für Naturkunde, Berlin;
Senckenburg Museum, Frankfurt am Main.

...e more than one
... number is listed for
...ic, the **bold**
...bers show you where
...d the main pages.

ISBN 0-439-32680-X